EMMAUS
The Way of Faith

EMMAUS: *The Way of Faith*

Emmaus: The Way of Faith is a resource designed to help churches welcome people into the Christian faith and the life of the Church. Emmaus has three stages:

Contact *– a simple guide for church members and leaders, exploring ways of beginning evangelism through listening and building relationships.*

Nurture *– a flexible 15-session course for evangelism and nurture that can be used with groups or with individuals and can form the core for outreach and mission in any local church.*

Growth *– 15 short courses for groups, spanning four books, concerning different aspects of the Christian faith. The growth courses can be used by any church group, but they are specifically designed for those wanting to go on growing in Christian discipleship after baptism, confirmation or some other adult declaration of faith.*

There are eight Emmaus books:

Introduction	*A vision for evangelism, nurture and growth in the local church*
Leading an Emmaus Group	*How to lead the Emmaus nurture and growth groups*
Stage 1: Contact	*Ideas for meeting people where they are*
Stage 2: Nurture	*A 15-session course for growing Christians*
Stage 3: Growth	*15 short courses for groups:*
Knowing God	*Four short courses for growing Christians:* *Living the Gospel* *Knowing the Father* *Knowing Jesus* *Come, Holy Spirit*
Growing as a Christian	*Five short courses for growing Christians:* *Growing in prayer* *Growing in the scriptures* *Being Church* *Growing in worship – understanding the sacraments* *Life, death and Christian hope*
Christian Lifestyle	*Four short courses for growing Christians:* *Living images* *Overcoming evil* *Personal identity* *Called into life*
Your Kingdom Come	*Two courses for growing Christians:* *The Beatitudes* *The kingdom*

The Emmaus web site: www.natsoc.org.uk/emmaus

EMMAUS
The Way of Faith

Introduction

*A vision for evangelism,
nurture and growth in the local church*

Stephen Cottrell, Steven Croft
John Finney, Felicity Lawson and Robert Warren

Second edition

The National Society
*Leading Education
with a Christian Purpose*
Church House Publishing

The National Society/
Church House Publishing
Church House
Great Smith Street
London
SW1P 3NZ

ISBN 7151 4963 6

Published 1996 by The National Society/Church House Publishing and The
Bible Society.

Second edition published 2001 by National Society Enterprises Ltd.

Acknowledgements

Scripture quotations are from *The Revised Standard Version of the Bible*
copyright © 1989 by the Division of Christian Education of the National
Council of Churches in the USA. Used by permission. All Rights Reserved.

Our thanks to Kate Bruce for work on the material in Chapter 5 and to all
who have given us feedback and told us their stories.

Cover design by Leigh Hurlock
Printed in England by Halstan & Co. Ltd, Amersham, Bucks.

Contents

Preface

Emmaus: The Way of Faith is a means of welcoming people into the Christian faith and the life of the Church. It is rooted in an understanding of evangelism, nurture and discipleship modelled on the example of Jesus as told in the story of the Emmaus road.

Emmaus: The Way of Faith enables the Church to:

●   *Pattern its life around Christ's call to make disciples.*

●   *Build relationships with those outside the Church.*

●   *Accompany enquirers on their journey of faith.*

●   *Bring new Christians to maturity.*

Emmaus does not come from any single Christian tradition. It has been inspired by the recent renewal of interest in the catechumenate as an accompanied journey into faith. Traditionally, the catechumen was someone who was being taught the rudiments of Christianity. Today, the catechumenate (meaning simply 'the teaching process') is a process of enquiry, instruction and transformation as an individual encounters the living Christ through his body, the Church.

The *Emmaus* nurture material began its life as a course developed in one parish church in the Diocese of Wakefield and has been widely used throughout the UK and in different parts of the world in churches of various traditions and denominations. In this new format the material has been revised and developed in the light of its extensive use.

This booklet gives an introduction to *Emmaus*. It gives a vision for evangelism, nurture and growth in the local church and provides practical ideas on how to move forward. A full list of the *Emmaus* materials can be found on page ii and details of the authors are on page 63.

Foreword

Emmaus: The Way of Faith is exactly what it says it is. Drawing upon the experience of the disciples 'on the way' with the risen Lord, this exciting programme of contact, nurture and growth is firmly based on the understanding that the coming to faith in Christ is a journey.

Here is a programme for churches of any and every shade of Christian tradition that seek to provide the necessary resources both to nurture and deepen the faith of those already on the way, as well as enabling the drawing into Christian faith and discipleship of those who come new and fresh to it. It represents the practical outworking of the *On the Way* report on the catechumenate, but will also be of great value outside the Church of England.

The real strength of what is contained in this introductory book, together with the course programme, is that it has emerged from the fresh and green shoots of the 'missionary' Diocese of Wakefield, where five different people coming from differing traditions found themselves journeying together in their engagement with the mission entrusted by God to his Church. Here is a rich resource greatly needed, which will surely transform and renew the lives both of individuals and of churches and congregations, so that we may more effectively live Christ's risen life and share the good news with others. In short *Emmaus: The Way of Faith* is very good news indeed!

The Most Reverend David Hope
The Archbishop of York

1
On the road –
an overview of the material

For most people, becoming a Christian is like a journey. *Emmaus: The Way of Faith* is a programme for helping churches help people make that journey. Like Jesus on the Emmaus road we are seeking to accompany people on a way that leads to the fullness of life.

At first sight the size of *Emmaus* and the number of books involved can all seem rather daunting. Actually *Emmaus* is very simple. There are three stages, with different material available for each stage.

Stage One: Contact

A book on making contact and building relationships

Stage Two: Nurture

A 15-session course

Stage Three: Growth

15 short courses for ongoing growth and discipleship

Figure 1: The three stages of *Emmaus*

This chapter gives an overview and description of each section and shows you how it all fits together.

1 Contact

Making contacts and building relationships is vital to any church concerned to communicate the Christian gospel to those outside the faith. The journey begins with people where they are in their ordinary daily life and takes seriously their questions, fears and aspirations. Like Jesus on the Emmaus road we meet people where they are and listen to their questions and needs. It is not sufficient simply to sit within our church services and meetings and wait for people to come to us. We must turn our focus outward: becoming missionary congregations, venturing beyond our own boundaries and serving the communities around us. This is the pattern Jesus set and calls us to follow.

Some churches may not need any help with this part of the process but many will. The 'making contact' part of the *Emmaus* material consists of a short, simple book entitled *Contact*, on how a local congregation with limited resources can begin to reach out to those around in terms of the relationships of church members. It describes the different projects the church may undertake to serve the community and a whole range of different 'stepping stones' which can be built to help people cross the often very wide gulf between the Church and the wider community. *Contact* is full of very practical ideas. It focuses on what kind of new things can be done and also on how the everyday service most churches provide for those around can become opportunities to help people move on in faith.

Contact is written not just for those in church leadership, ordained and lay. It is for every member of a congregation to read, digest and, if possible, study together, either as part of an ongoing group or as a special church project, perhaps in Lent. A four-session study guide is provided with the material.

2 Nurture

This begins when an individual, or a group, starts to explore the Christian life in more depth and seriousness. You could say that the contact stage of *Emmaus* ends when someone expresses a desire to find out more about the Christian faith. Like Jesus on the Emmaus road we aim to break open the Scriptures and the traditions of the Church to show their relevance to life and to lead people to a living encounter with Jesus. As we shall see later, a group may include enquirers, the term we are using here for those beginning the journey, and committed Christians accompanying them on the way and refreshing their own faith.

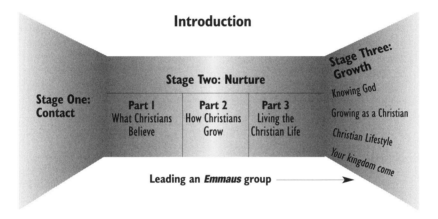

Figure 2: How the *Emmaus* books fit together and the different parts of the Nurture course

This is the stage on the way of faith that will look the most familiar. At its core is the following 15-session course covering the basics of Christian life and faith:

PART 1 WHAT CHRISTIANS BELIEVE

PART 2 HOW CHRISTIANS GROW

PART 3 LIVING THE CHRISTIAN LIFE

Some approaches to introducing the Christian faith have taken a more open-ended approach to the idea of syllabus and instruction. Some groups have had no syllabus at all, setting their own agenda for every session. Clearly there is a tension between the need to share and pass on the Christian tradition in a fairly formal way, and the need to foster an open dialogue with that tradition so that new Christians can appropriate and express the faith. In this stage of the *Emmaus* material we have taken the more systematic approach. We believe that the appropriate point for letting the enquirer set the agenda completely is first contact. Jesus says on the Emmaus road, 'What is it you have been talking about as you walk along?' This must always be the tone of our initial contact; an evangelism clearly rooted in love. After this, as people decide to explore more, they need a firm foundation in the basics of the faith before they are really able to develop a dialogue with it. This stage encourages exploration and provides plenty of opportunities for people to deal with their questions. But it does not back away from a basic grounding in the faith.

Although 15 sessions are provided for the *Emmaus* course, they can be tackled in any order. Some sessions can be omitted and others added or extended to suit the needs of the local church and those who are part of the group. It is important to note that the 15 sessions are arranged in 3 blocks. One of the ways that many churches use the *Emmaus* nurture material is in these three separate steps, at the end of each section inviting people to consider going a bit further. Later on you will also see that there is some helpful liturgical material that can be used to mark these steps of growth into faith.

The course includes a Leaders' Guide, a practical introduction to using the material, and handouts for group members, which can be photo-copied and used in any order. Our aim has been to produce inexpensive, flexible material, which each parish can adapt to its own needs. The Leaders' Guide also gives extensive notes on gathering a group together. This provides the link with the contact material. All the material has been very widely piloted by a number of churches and in nearly all cases the sessions have been led by lay people after a minimal amount of training. The *Emmaus* support book, *Leading an Emmaus Group*, will, of course, be very helpful here in training and supporting group leaders.

COMPANIONS ALONG THE WAY

One of the aims of *Emmaus* is to involve the whole church community in the process of initiation. There are various ways in which this can be done, but chief among them is the involvement of ordinary Christians in the whole nurture process. A good way of expressing this is to invite members of the existing congregation to act as sponsors to those people beginning the nurture stage.

There is no need to be frightened of the word 'sponsor'. The task of this person is simply to befriend and accompany the person beginning the nurture course. This can be done in different ways. One of the best is for the sponsor to go with the enquirer to the different sessions of the nurture stage. The group will therefore be made up of committed Christians and seekers. It does not have to be this way – the sponsor could remain in the background – but whatever happens it is an *Emmaus* road model of an accompanied journey.

The chief role of the sponsor is to pray for the enquirer and to be a point of contact for them when they do come to church. So often people finding out about faith know hardly anyone in the church, and if the only other people on the course are the vicar and other enquirers this will not help them to feel that they belong. And helping people feel they belong, and are valued and important, is as important as helping them to believe. Very often you will not have one without the other. The sponsors may also have a role in the special services of welcome that can mark the stages of the journey.

Many churches find it helpful not to use the word 'sponsor' at all. It can be a little off-putting for the person involved, not to mention the person being sponsored! Many churches simply say that their way of doing things is to involve the congregation by inviting people to take part in the course, and support and befriend those finding out about faith. An alternative word is 'companions', which originally meant 'those who take bread together'.

The Leaders' Guide for the nurture material contains a fuller description of the role sponsors can play; a handout that can be photocopied and given to sponsors; and an outline preparation meeting for people considering this ministry.

CELEBRATIONS ALONG THE WAY

These are services that mark the different stages of the journey. Although they are optional, many churches have experimented with different services of this kind, and most have found them extremely beneficial. They can involve the whole congregation and enable the whole church to make a commitment to those on the journey. They also confirm the public character of Christian commitment in a world that wants to reduce it to a private option.

David Sanderson, in a special appendix to the report *On the Way*, lists the benefits these special services bring:

● The congregation is included in the ministry to new members.

● The potential new members are brought to the attention of the congregation.

● The services mark the progress of the new member.

● The symbolism of the services is part of the growth process.

● The new members are affirmed and accepted by the Church.

The following services are recommended for use as part of the *Emmaus* material. Examples of each service, and some ideas on how to use them, are also included with the Leaders' Guide to the nurture stage. Similar material has been prepared by the Church of England Liturgical Commission and is available as a GS Misc Paper (GS Misc 530; not authorized for liturgical use). As far as possible we have tried to make the *Emmaus* material compatible with the work of the Commission.

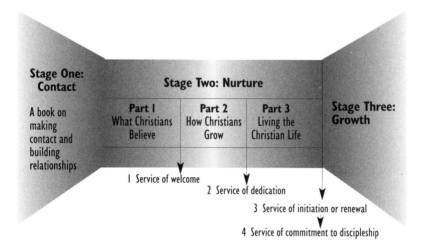

Figure 3: How the services fit into the nurture stage

A service of welcome

This would normally occur part of the way through the nurture stage, as some enquirers make a definite commitment to go forward towards initiation.

A service of dedication

This would take place when most of the preparation is complete and just prior to initiation. It could be used as part of a public service or as part of a special quiet day or preparation evening for a baptism or confirmation service.

A service of renewal

This would be instead of, or alongside, a service of baptism or confirmation, and would be especially for those who have already been baptized and confirmed.

A service of commitment to discipleship

This would take place after the service of initiation or renewal. It could be for all those about to embark upon the growth stage of *Emmaus*. The service could be used simply for those who are to be part of groups or it could be an act of worship for the whole congregation on a particular Sunday of the year.

By initiation here we mean baptism and/or confirmation. The writers of *Emmaus* are all Anglicans, yet we have tried to write for the whole Church. We believe that the *Emmaus* material can be used by all Christian churches and can therefore be preparation for all sorts of initiation.

Each church using the material will need to decide how to use these special services – and which of them to use. One difficulty for Anglican churches is that it is not always possible to plan a confirmation service at a convenient moment in the year. However, if the special services outlined here are used in the local church, it is not as important that the confirmation itself takes place in a person's own parish.

We would strongly recommend that each local church plans its own pattern for Christian initiation each year. Think about what is best for your church rather than trying to gear everything to when the bishop happens to be in the area.

3   Growth

The growth stage of *Emmaus* aims to help people discover their own vocation and ministry and have a share in the apostolic life of the whole Church. Every Christian is called to share in God's mission of love to the world. The emphasis, therefore, is on formation rather than information. Too often we are content with letting growth come to a halt after a very short period of nurture and instruction leading to initiation. The aim of the growth stage is to lead people beyond themselves to a new way of being human. This is the part of *Emmaus* that most challenges traditional models of preparing people for church membership. It also carries the most potential for facilitating major change in the whole culture of the Church. If the bottleneck is the stunted growth of so many churchgoing Christians, then the active discipling of all who come to faith will have a direct and dramatic effect on our mission to the world.

The growth stage is published in four books consisting of 15 short courses of between 4 and 6 sessions each. The starting-off points are the sessions of the nurture stage, but the aim is to go deeper and allow for much more sharing and exploration. It is not necessary to do the courses in order. In fact it is not necessary to do all the courses! Because every church has different priorities, it is essential for each church and group to plot its own course. It would also be rather daunting to say that the growth stage consisted of 60 sessions! Think of the nurture stage as a set menu and the growth stage as *à la carte*!

The important point is that growth does not stop. Commitment leads somewhere, and wherever possible it is focused outwards in mission. Each church is encouraged to develop its own pattern using the resources provided. But a church or group may plan to cover all the material over a three- or four-year period, thus ensuring that all new Christians receive a thorough grounding in the faith.

GROUPS OR COURSES?

An important decision for each church to make at this stage is whether to run the material for the growth stage in ongoing groups or short, one-off courses. Although both options are possible, ongoing groups are preferable in most cases.

Most parishes have the resources to run only one course at a time. Some can only run one course of any kind each year. The most vital course for any church to run is the one for nurture. It will open up the possibility of a continuous stream of new adult disciples coming into the congregation.

How can material concerning ongoing growth fit into the life of a church? The best way is to encourage the members from each nurture group to stay together afterwards and engage with some of the courses in the growth section (perhaps mixed in with material from other sources). Each small group, under lay leadership, would then decide for themselves which subjects to tackle and in what order. The role of the clergy or ministers would be to oversee and support the life of the groups and, most importantly, to support the lay leaders in their ministry of building up and equipping the body of Christ.

Some of the sponsors in the original nurture group may wish to stay with the new group as it forms. Others may wish to go back to their original 'growth' groups, or to have a break and then sponsor someone else through the nurture stage.

Leadership of groups for the nurture stage should be seen as a specialist ministry. St Paul refers to those given the task of laying the foundations as 'master builders'. It takes time, practice and some training and experience to become skilled at leading groups of this kind. Normally, we would advise the key nurture group leaders in a church not to take the group forward to the growth stage but to hold themselves in reserve for the next nurture group. This means you will need to have possible leaders for the growth stage of a group's life already in place (or at least in mind) as a nurture group begins. In general, leading a group through the growth materials requires less specialized knowledge and skill than leading a nurture group: it is much more of an experience of discovery and sharing together.

Over the course of several years using the *Emmaus* material, a church following this pattern will be seeking to establish:

- A nurture course, repeated regularly and led by specialized leaders.

- A growing network of small groups (or occasional courses) enabling Christians to go on growing and being equipped to live out their baptism. These groups will be open to new members and lay led. Each will follow the growth materials in a different order, decided by the groups themselves. Over time, hopefully, each group will also become involved in mission and faith sharing as part of its ongoing life.

This structure also has the advantage of continually building up community. As a local church grows in numbers, the capacity for pastoral care will continually increase.

Churches that decide not to attempt to set up a structure of ongoing groups for learning, mission and pastoral care (or try it and find it does not work) will need to offer the growth materials as special courses during the year. Assuming that your church can probably only run one kind of course at a time, the year will need to be carefully planned so that the growth courses fit in well with the ongoing and regularly repeated nurture course.

An excellent way to plan is to work around the cycle of the liturgical year. Two possibilities are given below.

Example 1

- Begin to think about gathering a nurture group in October (that may mean leaving October and November clear of major events in the life of the Church – gathering a group takes time and energy).

- Start the group just before Advent (making sure you have at least six meetings before Christmas). Hold your first service of welcome at Epiphany time and then aim for the main services of initiation at or around Easter.

- One or two growth courses can then be held over the months from Easter to September, perhaps involving the wider congregation as well as those who have been part of the nurture course in the previous year.

Example 2

- Begin the nurture group each year in October, leaving the summer months for gathering the group together. Hold the initial service of welcome in Advent and the main initiation services at Epiphany.

- Lent could then see a range of different groups offered to the whole congregation, including the new members, with each group tackling a different part of the growth material.

- The period from Easter to Pentecost could be left unplanned to give people space to absorb what they have learned with a second batch of courses offered after Pentecost.

Both examples assume the church is fairly small and is beginning the process by running just one nurture group each year. If your church is larger and/or already has a great many contacts, you may need to run more than one nurture group as resources allow.

There is fluidity to the whole process. The contact stage suggests how each church may develop its outreach. This leads to the formation of the nurture stage, from which it is hoped many will come to faith and join the Church. The growth stage again allows each church to be different. In this way we trust that the *Emmaus* material will be helpful to churches across the spectrum of traditions and denominations. There is no one right way of doing things, and churches are to be encouraged to find their own best route.

Here is a list of the growth courses:

STAGE 3: GROWTH – KNOWING GOD

Living the Gospel

Knowing the Father

Knowing Jesus

Come, Holy Spirit

STAGE 3: GROWTH – GROWING AS A CHRISTIAN

Growing in prayer

Growing in the Scriptures

Being Church

Growing in worship – understanding the sacraments

Life, death and Christian hope

STAGE 3: GROWTH – CHRISTIAN LIFESTYLE

Living images

Overcoming evil

Personal identity

Called into life

STAGE 3: GROWTH – YOUR KINGDOM COME

The Beatitudes

The kingdom

More details about each course can be found at the beginning of the relevant growth book. Like the nurture material, each book has leaders' notes and photocopiable handouts for group members.

It is also worth noting that one of the growth courses – 'Living the Gospel', to be found at the beginning of the first growth book, *Knowing God* – can be used at the beginning of the *Emmaus* material or at the end! It can be used with existing groups in every church or with special study groups to encourage and build skills in sharing faith through relationships. With the exception of this course about sharing our faith, there is a general progression through the growth stage from concentrating on a person's own understanding, personal discipleship and identity near the beginning to a focus on being called and commissioned to play your part in the mission of God in the world.

The growth stage does not really end at all. More could be added to it. The most important thing is that every new Christian initiated into the faith realizes that faith is always a journey. There is no point in this life when we can say we have arrived.

THE JOURNEY OF FAITH

The overall pattern of the *Emmaus* material can therefore be seen as three stages (see Figure 1). Some people will begin with contact, pass through nurture and move on to growth. Others may join at different points. 'Completing' the three stages is not the end of the journey. The life-long process of growth in discipleship and vocation continues as we join with God in building the kingdom on earth. One of the ways in which this bears fruit is in a fresh and consistent Christian witness to those who are beginning The Way. As people see Christian faith in action they begin to ask questions of what life is all about. And so new journeys to faith begin.

2

A pilgrim people – the principles behind *Emmaus*

Emmaus has not been created in a vacuum. Rather it is the fruit of consciously seeking to learn from the whole history of the Church's work of initiating people into faith in Christ. It has also sought to draw insights from  across the world today. It then seeks to rework and apply those insights to contemporary culture. Such engagement with the whole Christian heritage, of helping people on the journey of faith, is full of rich rewards. In part this is because the context of the Church in the first few centuries of the Christian era is similar in many ways to today's world.

We, like they, live in a world of rapid change and a ferment of religious activity, together with a declining faith in the contemporary gods and a search for something that makes sense of life and gives meaning, hope and an awareness of being connected with 'ultimate reality'.

Our modern world has broken down life into little compartments, analysing everything from the cosmos to the kiss. The whole of life has been fragmented. No wonder, therefore, that there is such a search for meaning and something that 'makes sense of life'. Seeing faith as a journey helps in that process of bringing life together. It draws together the varied strands of pre-evangelism, evangelism, nurture, discipleship, church (as the community of faith) and kingdom. It is that integration on which *Emmaus* is built and which it seeks to foster.

Seeing faith as a journey is not a new insight. Indeed it can be seen as the oldest one of all, for Christianity was called 'The Way' before it was called anything else; and Christians were called 'followers of the Way' before they were called Christians (see The Acts of the Apostles).

This sense of journey was fundamental in the idea of the catechumenate developed by the Church in the first three centuries. The catechumenate (meaning simply 'teaching pattern') was often a three-year process of equipping new Christians to grasp the nature of faith. It helped them work out the often costly implications of following Christ in the whole of life. Several of the authors of *Emmaus* have studied the ways in which the Early Church did lead people not only to faith, but also on into maturity of discipleship, which – for some – led all the way to courageous martyrdom.

Near to our own time, the spread of the faith through John Wesley's evangelistic ministry was in large measure due to the work he did in establishing people through the weekly 'class meeting'. These 'class meetings' were specifically and consciously seeking to restore to the Church of the eighteenth century the insights of the early catechumenates, applying them to that particular historical and social setting.

We also want to acknowledge the debt we owe to the pioneering work of the Catholic Church since Vatican II in developing and implementing *The Rite of Christian Initiation of Adults* (RCIA). Many Catholic churches have found the material of RCIA to be not only effective in initiation of newcomers, but also in renewing the faith of all church members. Churches in other denominations have valued this material and drawn on it in the development of their own material.

The journey, or 'process', approach to communicating the faith has been one of the major developments in the life of the Church in recent decades. Without any overall coordination or planning, a whole series of resources has sprung up which helps people to explore the faith over a period of time. In addition to RCIA, such materials as *Emmaus, Alpha, Credo, The Y Course*, etc., have all been developed to meet this need and express this desire of the Church to take time to enable people to engage with the faith over a period of weeks.

In 1995 The House of Bishops of the Church of England produced a report entitled *On the Way*, which drew attention to this 'integrated approach to Christian initiation', reflected on the issues involved and gave points about best practice in this area of the Church's mission.

As authors of this material, we are conscious of working within the whole Christian tradition of initiation. We are convinced that Christians from all denominations and traditions have much to learn from each other in helping people to become followers of The Way. The following principles have been important to us in preparing the material.

1	*Entry into faith is a process of discovery*
2	*A process best practised as an accompanied journey*
3	*A process that affects our whole lives*
4	*Effective initiation affects the life of the whole Church*

I Entry into faith is a process of discovery

For much of the recent history of the Church, entry into faith has been seen as a crisis moment in a person's life. Hence the use of terms like 'making a decision for Christ'. There is an important truth in such an approach. However, what the Church has been discovering in recent years is that decisions arise much more out of a process of exploring, questioning, experiencing and reflecting, which often takes several years. The research of John Finney, published in *Finding Faith Today*, established that most people coming to faith do so over a period of months and typically over a period of several years.

This awareness of the process behind any step forward in faith fits well with modern educational thinking. That thinking identifies a natural 'learning cycle' through which we all go. It is made up of the process 'experience – reflection – action'. We experience something (for example a draught around our head) that prompts us to reflect (on where it is coming from) and results in our taking appropriate action (getting up and shutting the window).

At a more profound level, the apostle Peter *experienced* Jesus as someone who did not seem to fit any category into which people wanted to put him – teacher, John the Baptist returned to life or one of the prophets. As he *reflected* on this, he had a moment of revelation that enabled him to *take the step* of acknowledging that Jesus was 'the Christ'. He was learning not just information, but a way of understanding reality. He integrated this into his experience of life in such a way that he was transformed in the very process of that learning.

This understanding of faith as a process, a journey, lies behind the development of the *Emmaus* material. It is designed to help in the work of assisting people to encounter God in Christ and to relate that discovery to the whole of life.

A PROCESS OF DISCOVERY RATHER THAN DICTATION

Because the emphasis is on discovery, it is important that those using this material should be careful to minimize a teacher/pupil style. *Emmaus* is not intended to be used as material that the 'teacher' (who is the 'expert') uses to tell the person seeking after faith (the 'ignorant') what the truth is. Some element of telling – both in the sense of 'pointing the way' and in giving necessary information – will be needed. However, much more important, continuing the journey theme, is that we walk together 'in the Way of Christ', discovering together on that journey more of the God in whom we place our faith. One of us may be more mature in years and in the faith, but true maturity is always open to learn and to listen, and to see the faith afresh through the eyes of a comparative newcomer.

Moreover, so much of the faith puts us all on the same level. The retired bishop or missionary is by no means necessarily ahead of the giddy teenager, when it comes to repentance, faith or the courage to obey.

So this material is essentially designed around the principle of *discovery* rather than *instruction*. This makes it easier to use in the small group setting as the 'leader' does not need to give instruction or know all the answers (see *Leading an Emmaus Group*). In larger group settings some brief input does work best (usually not more than 20 minutes) before people break into small groups to work through the material.

2 A process best practised as an accompanied journey

The assumption already made is that initiation takes place not so much through open notebooks but through open lives. There is a sense of adventure and exploration for all involved. Essential to this approach is our own openness to grow and learn. Being alongside another in their journey of faith needs to be done in a spirit of mutual learning. Such learning is a two-way partnership not a one-way production line.

Another picture is that of the midwife, bringing new life to birth. Paul wrote to the Galatians: 'my little children, for whom I am again in the pain of childbirth until Christ is formed in you' (Galatians 4.19). He is gloriously free in his use of the picture, casting himself in the role of the one in labour, but the Galatians as the ones in whom Christ will be born. The work of being alongside another, exploring and discovering the faith, is like midwifery for it is about bringing forth new life in a person. Our task is to be there to assist others in their discovery of God. How gently, clearly and skilfully Jesus did that with the disciples on the road to *Emmaus*.

The midwife is not the one who causes the new life to be formed in the person; that is done by grace and by revelation through the Holy Spirit. Ours is the humbler task of helping that life to find expression. Doing so will raise questions about how far Christ is being formed, and being given expression, in us. The sense of walking together, of companionship and mutual openness, and the need to learn together, is essential to true initiation. *Emmaus: The Way of Faith* has been developed to aid just this kind of mutual learning and encouragement.

3   A process that affects our whole lives

Pendulums have a habit of swinging. In grasping the insight about entry into faith as a process, it would be easy to go too far and reject any notion of 'crisis' or moments of decision. Yet a journey, like any process, is made up of a whole series of decisions. The way of discipleship is much more like a walk in the hills, where choices about which way to go are constantly being made, rather than like a train journey, where only one decision is made about the destination and then everything happens automatically (on a good day!).

The faith journey is not accomplished without the making of choices and decisions. The scriptural term here is that of *metanoia*, usually translated 'repentance'. However, the idea is much richer than our notion of repentance as owning up to wrong doings. A better translation is 'changing your mind'. It is more an attitude of 'Ah, now I see', which, by enabling us to see something in a new light, changes how we handle life. Learning to walk is a form of this profound turning. Once we grasp how it is done, and that it can be done by us, we are off exploring a new world and a whole new dimension to living. Jesus came to call people for just this reason when he proclaimed the coming of God's kingdom: 'repent and believe the good news'.

That change is seen as a profound reworking of a person's whole life. It means seeing life from a whole new perspective, and therefore handling it differently. Such a change is well illustrated when a couple fall in love and decide to get married. It is not only a wonderful experience in itself, but it changes everything else in their lives: how they spend their time and their money, what they consider to be important, where they will make sacrifices. Such a relationship is life-changing. So it is to discover ourselves as part of the Bride of Christ.

The illustration of falling in love helps us see how change and process work together. Making a proposal, or getting married, does not take much time but its impact on our lives lasts for a lifetime. The choice leads to an unending process of change. So too with baptism; the act itself takes little time. Rightly understood, its impact lasts a lifetime. As the Catholic Rite of Initiation of Adults (RCIA) put it:

> *Few Christians are ever fully evangelised,*
> *all our lives we need the power of the gospel*
> *to transform us.*
>
> RCIA *Study Book*, p.14.

A TRANSFORMED LIFE

There are three levels of communication in an effective process of initiation. Imparting *information* is the first level. Particularly in today's world, we should not assume that people are familiar with our church or Christian terminology; or that words we use necessarily mean the same thing. At the most basic level, when someone talks about 'God' they do not necessarily mean the one revealed as 'the God and Father of us all' through the revelation in Christ.

The second level of communication is that of *formation* – the shaping of our lives to reflect the truth we see and the faith we hold. Again, this is why a period of time is needed so that people have the opportunity to assimilate and apply the faith to their daily living. It is important to see that this is a key task in accompanying others on the journey of faith; namely, helping them to work out, and then live out, the implications of their baptism. The Reformers of the sixteenth century, such as Martin Luther, spoke of 'improving' or 'proving' our baptism. By this they meant that the Christian faith is a life to live not just a creed to assent to. Which is where accompanying people on the journey of faith is so vital. It is the task of sharing our own joys and struggles in living out the faith we profess. That is, telling the story of our own present 'formation'.

The third level of communication is that of *transformation*. This is the ultimate goal of the good news of Jesus Christ, to change our way of seeing God, life and ourselves and thus changing the way we live our lives. We see it in the New Testament taking place in people such as Peter and Paul, whose lives, sense of vocation and self-understanding were profoundly transformed through their encounter with Christ.

We cannot transform another person, but we can assist in the process, though we are unlikely to do so if we ourselves are not also engaging in the continual process of transformation in our own lives.

There are a number of areas of our lives where such transformation is needed and can be expected to take place. In using the *Emmaus* materials, it helps to bear in mind these areas as listed below. They are like places that the journey of faith will take us all through as we seek to live out our baptism.

Transforming our lives through . . .

- spirituality
- self-acceptance
- changed character
- community
- worldview
- lifestyle
- mission

SPIRITUALITY

Spirituality is about how we engage with God. It affects the whole of life and our view of it, but finds particular and focused expression in the practice of prayer, meditation and the worship of God. Spirituality is about our knowing God, and our being known by him. All that we do to help people explore and follow the Christian way, to help them encounter God through corporate worship, in the life of prayer and in the midst of life, is a foundational resource. No amount of information about God can substitute for the personal knowledge, the true knowing of God. Our task is not just, for example, to talk about prayer, but to pray together.

SELF-ACCEPTANCE

Self-acceptance is one of the greatest gifts of the good news in Christ, and one of the clearest evidences of the life of faith at work in a person's life. Awareness of God brings us to an awareness of ourselves. Too easily that is seen in a negative light as awareness of what is wrong with us. The first impact of the gospel is the discovery that we are loved and accepted, that God delights in us. This was the discovery the prodigal son, and so many who encountered Jesus in his lifetime, made. It is a glorious part of the good news that many take years to grasp.

The reason we find it hard to believe, accept and receive God's love for us is that much of our self-understanding comes from our family nurture, and from the self-image given by our parents. This often needs healing. Scripture and church tradition point to the value of receiving a new name. Abram becomes Abraham, Simon becomes Peter, Saul becomes Paul. Each in their different way discovers a whole, new and more positive self-understanding through encounter with God. This was the original significance of the baptismal name. Though taking on a new name in baptism is rarely a practical option today, it is important for the new believer to discover and embrace a 'redeemed self-understanding'. The Growth module on personal identity particularly addresses this subject.

CHANGED CHARACTER

Changed character points to the fact that we are always in a process of becoming. While personal identity addresses who we are, changed character points to the fact that we are 'becoming persons'. The process of becoming takes place through choices we make.

Our natural concern is often that God will change the circumstances in which we live. God's concern is with our character as shaped through circumstances and our response to them. The Beatitudes are the shape of the character of Christ, which God intends to create in the life of the Church. There is a progression in them from the openness of vulnerability (poor in spirit), to strength in vulnerability (blessed are the persecuted). This occurs whenever the believer follows Christ by seeking to overcome evil with good. This process of being formed, sometimes on 'the anvil of adversity', needs to be grasped if we are to hear God in testing times, and be of help to others going through fiery trials. Effective nurture works with people as they wrestle with difficult choices, and helps them find the resources to make choices from a place of faith and openness to the will and purposes of God.

COMMUNITY

Community belongs to the very nature of God – as Trinity. This is one of the reasons why entry into the Christian faith has, down the centuries, so often taken place in small groups. Such groups enable the enquirer to experience Christ among his people, and to experience the process of a group of people becoming church. Effective initiation introduces the new believer to the dynamic of living in love – a giving-and-receiving openness to others. This 'dwelling together in love' is what the gospel both calls us to and equips us for. This is essentially counterculture living. The *Emmaus* material is designed to assist in the process of developing a community that lives in the truth of the two great commandments to love God and to love others.

Belonging is one of the great fruits of believing.

WORLDVIEW

Worldview describes the way we see reality. For example, we in the Western world have a scientific worldview. We approach and interpret our experience of life from within a culture that looks for a natural cause-and-event explanation of all that happens to us. We treat all new information with analysis and suspicion. 'Prove it' is a creed close to the heart of our culture. There is much validity in such an approach, but it also has serious limitations. It closes our minds to experiences of beauty and wonder, the capacity to create and dream. It closes us off from the world of the spirit and of angels. This scientific worldview can only 'see' material things and the market process and can stifle the creative, imaginative and artistic side of our humanity. It applies that grid to the filtering of all that it sees.

The Christian worldview, as expressed in the Scriptures, creeds and traditions of the Church, points to an understanding of the world created by a loving personal God and upheld within his gracious, eternal purposes. Our lives gain significance from participating in his purposes for the whole of the created order – 'his-story'. This does not mean that we set aside a scientific view of the world or see it as an enemy to be fought. However, we need to let our faith challenge the limitations and blind spots in the worldview around us.

LIFESTYLE

Lifestyle has to do with the way we handle our lives. It concerns the way we treat other people, our attitude to material possessions, our (often unconscious) motives and priorities. Our lifestyle reflects the values and priorities of our lives. The message of Christ needs to engage with the lifestyle we have adopted. We cannot allow the faith to be just a matter of 'private religion'. The gospel calls us to live life in a way that reflects the things that we see matter in the life of Jesus.

MISSION

Mission is the calling of all who name the name of Christ. To be initiated is nothing less than to join in with God's mission in the world. Initiation is, ultimately, into the kingdom and not simply church membership.

Baptism is 'the ordination of the laity'. Christ's triple ministry of prophet, priest and king is to be lived out by the Church as a community in the midst of its life in the world. The true test of effective initiation is not so much what sort of church members it produces, as what sorts of human beings emerge from the process. What sort of effect do they have on those with whom they live and work? What is their contribution to the world as it is being gathered up into God's purposes in Christ?

4 Effective initiation affects the life of the whole Church

It would be quite possible to take the *Emmaus* material and use it to run some helpful and effective groups. It can be used with groups exploring the Christian faith, with confirmation groups and with nurture groups for new Christians. The material can also work well with established church members and established home groups, acting as a refresher course to remind them about the nature and content of our faith.

However, just to use the material like that would be to miss most of its real worth. It would be to use it at something like 20 per cent of its potential. The real value of this material can only be discovered when a church shapes its life around the process of initiation. Only when a church builds initiation into its way of life (and nature of operating) will it become the sort of church into which it is healthy to be initiated.

The Church in the first three centuries of the Christian era saw initiation in just this way. Out of this understanding came the idea of the Christian year, beginning in Advent with celebration of Christ's coming, leading on into the accounts of the birth (Christmas) and revelation of Christ (Epiphany), and so on to consider his life (Lent) and, in particular, his death (Holy Week) and resurrection (Easter), and the outpouring of the Spirit (Pentecost). Each year the newcomers and the faithful were reminded of the great story of Christ of which we have been made a part through baptism. Through it, they experienced the truth that because the Christian is 'in Christ', we experience his life at work in us. Every Eucharist identifies with his death and resurrection, every baptism reminds us that we have been incorporated into Christ, every Pentecost that we have received of God's Spirit.

Although part of it took place in small groups, initiation was built firmly into the weekly and annual liturgy of the Church. This was done through a whole series of rites or special services. Those services reminded the whole Church of its own baptism, and of the faith into which it had been initiated. Modern examples have been included in the *Emmaus* material.

The teaching method of the Early Church was thoroughly modern. They did not rely on any one method. They did teach from Scripture, though it was primarily of a devotional nature. They used rites and liturgies, symbols and actions (such as the 'presentation' of the Lord's Prayer and the Creed to candidates during Sunday worship). They used sponsors and the friendship of those who accompanied the enquirers. They used all the spiritual resources at their command from prayer and retreats to exorcism and anointing, as well as testimony. Wise counsel and spiritual direction also formed part of their rich set of ingredients for the work of initiation.

The *Emmaus* material includes many suggestions about ways of using symbols and actions to engage with the spiritual dimension and to enable enquirers to tell their stories. Those who use it are encouraged to use as rich a mixture of ways of communicating as possible.

Undoubtedly, the most fruitful way to make use of this material is to rework the whole inner life of the Church around the theme of the faith community. Once we see that the purpose of the Church is to live the gospel, we can make connections between the work of initiation and the whole life of the Church. If our calling is to live in and out of the resources of the gospel, then how we worship, how we relate together and how we engage with the communities around us will all be affected by such a conviction. So will the work of initiation, for we will be seeking help for people to grasp, and to be grasped by, the gospel, and to find grace through it.

THE INITIATING CHURCH LETS US LIVE OUT OUR BAPTISM

A church that is a real initiating community will not only put its energies into that work, but will allow the witness of those coming to faith to challenge continually the way the church handles its life. Does the way we relate to one another express the outworking of what we say in our nurture groups about 'dwelling together in love'? What is the Christian way of handling conflict? Is this modelled in the nurture group, and in the life of the church? Does what happens on Sunday serve and challenge the outworking of the faith by the whole church during the week? Do those exploring the faith engage with the sense of mission that is at the very heart of Christian faith?

It is a costly thing to reorder the life of any local church. It can also be enormously creative to reshape the life of the church around the outworking of our common baptism. By that baptism we have received the love and grace of God; we have a new identity through being called Christian. We have also been given a new 'family of origin', and a new purpose in life, namely participation in Christ's redemption of all creation through our working with him to overcome evil with good.

The *Emmaus* material is offered to the Church to enable it to help those exploring the faith, and those new in the faith, to discover what the knowledge of God is all about. Through it the life of the local church may become truly integrated and charged with the vital task of initiating newcomers to the faith. In this way the 'faith once delivered to the saints' can be passed on to the next generation. At the same time those young in the faith can continually recall the 'faithful' to be faith-filled and bear fruit in the knowledge of God.

3

The road to Emmaus – the biblical model

It is a hot afternoon on the first Easter day. Two of Jesus' followers, Cleopas and an unnamed companion, are leaving Jerusalem. We are not told why they are leaving; though it is reasonable to suppose that it might be for the same reason that the other disciples have locked themselves away. They are frightened that what has happened to Jesus will happen to them.

They are heading for Emmaus, a village about seven miles from Jerusalem. A good two hours' walk. However, their real destination is not a place on a map but a new experience of God, which is already forming in them as they walk along. In this respect they are already disciples. Like many people today who are outside the Church they have a sense of God, an intuitive understanding of right and wrong and a thirst for truth. Cleopas and his companion have been followers of Jesus and it is the strange events that have unfolded in Jerusalem over the previous couple of days that form the basis of their conversation.

In another respect they still have much to discover. They do not really know what it means to follow Christ. Perhaps, like so many others, they think you can separate the message from the messenger. Perhaps they have confined God's message to the world of ideas, without seeing it as a new orientation for the whole of life. Like all the disciples, they have yet to see that what God has done in Jesus Christ is the foundation stone of a new reality, and also a stumbling block for every other interpretation of human life. They know that Jesus lived and died. They do not yet know the *meaning of his life and death, nor do they yet know that God has raised him to new life.*

This understanding of what God has done in Christ can only be found when the road of their life converges with the road of the risen Christ: the Christ who now bears the marks of suffering love for all the world and every human person.

When this encounter takes place, however good their path has been to this point, they will be turned around. They are walking to Emmaus, but they are about to be pointed back to Jerusalem. The road to Emmaus will become the way of faith.

This story of encounter and conversion reveals the *Emmaus* way of evangelizing and nurturing people into the Christian life. At the heart of *Emmaus* is a longing to share the love of God in a way centred on the example given us by Jesus himself. We are seeking commitment, but understand that for most people in the mosaic of cultures and experiences that make up contemporary society, coming to faith will be a journey before it is an event.

I Contact

Figure 4: The Emmaus journey

As the two companions walk along, Jesus himself comes and walks at their side. They do not recognize him. Jesus conceals his identity. It is hard to overstress the significance of these few verses of Scripture. Jesus meets them where they are. He walks with them, even while they are going in the wrong direction! He listens before he speaks. His first words to them are: 'What are all these things you have been discussing as you walk along?'

If we understand this story as a model for evangelism and nurture, it is an approach staggeringly different from the way the Christian Church usually operates. Jesus' question stands in judgement on the quick fix, instant results, in or out proselytism that passes for evangelism in many churches.

Jesus performs an act of self-giving that is not looking for reward save the satisfaction of love freely given and the hope that love will be freely returned. After all, this is the first Easter day and Jesus could be forgiven a little triumphalism. His approach is the precise opposite. In order to preserve the possibility that love will be freely returned, his glory is veiled, his identity concealed.

This is the great scandal of the gospel that Paul often speaks of. God does not want us as slaves, mere puppets who could hardly refuse relationship with God if he were to disclose his hand in such a way that our freedom to respond would become irrelevant. But neither does he only want us as friends. It is our freedom, our precious responsibility for the way we live our lives, that makes us loveable. It is the deepest truth of our humanity; it is the image of God within us. We are not slaves to instinct. We are capable of tremendous creativity and love and also able to be held captive by the spoiling sin of our wrong choices. But God will not intervene in such a way that would destroy the delicate harmony of our freedom: then we would cease to be human. Always he must reveal his love to us in such a way that safeguards our ability to choose how we respond.

This is why the path of God's love begins in the womb of the Virgin Mary; a God emptied of power and sovereignty in order to know what it is to be human. He communicates love to humanity in the only way we could receive it and still be free. And this is why that love had also to embrace the cold wood of the cross. We are neither to be slaves, nor only friends, but co-heirs with Christ to the kingdom of heaven! This is the Christian gospel. It is this gospel the Church must share, and it must be shared with the same self-giving love of Jesus.

That is why Jesus' first words are a question not a statement. The Church finds it easy to give the impression that becoming a Christian is about gaining possession of a body of knowledge. Yet we know that becoming a Christian is actually about being in relationship with God through Jesus Christ, discovering our true inheritance and citizenship. We also know that many Christians suffer from stunted growth. They know a lot about God, but they do not really know God.

There is a longing for spiritual truth in our culture. This is not about knowledge, neither is it about bolting on to an existing worldview a few pious truths. This tendency has impoverished the Church for many generations. Our doctrine of God is of persons in communion. Therefore at the very heart of evangelism must be relationship. For this to be real, people's aspirations, needs and questions must be taken very seriously. People need to know it is all right to ask a question. People need to be encouraged to tell their story of what has happened on the road of their life. We are not just leading people to information, though this is important, but to transformation. People want to know God.

At the beginning, therefore, we must be prepared to go at their pace, in their direction, and, as far as possible, with their agenda and their questions. This can look like compromise. Wasn't Jesus endlessly accused of this by the religious people of his day? 'This man eats with tax-collectors and sinners.'

What it does demonstrate is tremendous love. Basil Hume has commented that judgement, properly understood, is telling the story of your life into the ear of an all-loving Father.

2 Nurture

And so a journey begins. Jesus accompanies Cleopas and his companion on their walk to Emmaus. They explain all that has happened to them and to the Jesus they had been following, and of their hope that he would be the one to set Israel free.

And there comes a point on the journey, though it will be different in every situation and with every person, when listening becomes dialogue and sharing faith becomes growth into faith.

Jesus starts to explain to them the true meaning of the Scriptures, of 'how it was necessary that the Christ should suffer before entering into his glory'.

Jesus even rebukes them. He has clearly built up a friendly relationship with them, and he is able to point out the weaknesses in what they are saying as well as affirming the strengths. The overall impression is one of great exhilaration: 'Were not our hearts burning within us while he talked with us on the road?'

A story that had been familiar is at last seen in its true light. Although in contemporary culture we cannot assume any familiarity with the Christian story, there will be a point when the sharing of the Christian story, perhaps for the first time, will lead to a proper understanding of the human story.

It is this that will lead to the turning around that is the first climax of this journey.

This journey has to lead somewhere. On the Emmaus road a process of nurture – an accompanied journey of sharing, instruction and explanation – leads to a dramatic revelation of Christ. It won't always be like this. Sometimes it is precisely the other way round. St Paul disappeared for three years after his encounter with Christ (Galatians 1.17-18). He went to grow and learn.

There must, however, be clear moments of recognition and commitment. For the two companions on the Emmaus road it is in the breaking of bread. This is of particular interest because it provides a balance between encounter with Jesus in his word (the journey on the road) and encounter with Christ in the sacrament (the supper at Emmaus). We need this balance to give us a full-blooded scriptural and catholic approach to evangelism and nurture. If we also look to the Eucharist as a model (Liturgy of the Word/Liturgy of the Sacrament) a third element becomes vital. This is the sharing of the peace – the recognition of the presence of Christ in his people. This belief under-girds all that is presented here – God's supreme revelation of himself is as a human person. The word is made flesh. Not a manifesto but a man. Not a message but a messenger. On the road to Emmaus Jesus begins by cherishing and respecting the humanity of those he comes alongside. When they recognize him as the risen Lord, all knowledge, and all that has gone before, is subsumed to the new relationship they enter into.

The great scholar Thomas Aquinas, towards the end of his life, received a wonderful revelation of Christ in glory. He later described his life's work, a vast library of theological writings, as so much straw compared to this one moment.

God is the evangelist. We must trust in his faithfulness that people will come to this moment of revelation. The story of the Emmaus road teaches us about God's evangelism, focuses our minds on the way Jesus approached people, and shows that our task is to be faithful witnesses, making contact with people on the road of their lives, and then faithfully accompanying them on a journey to faith. As we shall also see, with both the Emmaus road and the Eucharist there is another element – that of being commissioned for service.

Commitment is not seen as a separate stage, or even a definite point, in the *Emmaus* material. However, there is opportunity within the nurture stage to make a personal decision to follow Christ – at a time that is right for each individual – and a public decision to go forward to baptism, confirmation or a renewal of baptismal vows. There is therefore hope, and an expectation that the road will lead to commitment and membership of the Church.

3 Growth

The two companions discover the true direction of their lives. They discover that this journey is not going to end at Emmaus but Jerusalem. And so they set out that instant and return to Jerusalem to share what they have received.

There is always a tension in the Christian life between being a disciple, one who follows, and an apostle, one who is sent. So at the beginning of the gospel Jesus says 'follow' and at the end he says 'go'. We need to do both. One could say that having been properly nurtured, walking with Jesus on the road, Cleopas and his friend are able to become apostles, rushing back to Jerusalem to share their story. Here new life with Jesus leads naturally to witness and evangelism.

WELCOME AND LOVE

There are two other remarkable elements in the Emmaus story that are of relevance to a church that wants to take evangelism and nurture seriously: welcome and love.

When these two companions return to Jerusalem the eleven disciples welcome them. They are outsiders to this inner group, they are possibly even deserters, but they are still warmly welcomed into the household of faith.

In the main, the Church has an impoverished understanding of welcome. Often it is little more than smiling at people as they arrive at church. If the Christian gospel is about becoming co-heirs with Christ to eternal life – a new life that can begin here and now – then welcome is about adoption of new members into the household. These members will enjoy the same rights and privileges as everyone else, no matter what they have done in the past and no matter how junior their membership.

It has often been observed that many churches do not grow because they do not want to. What this means is that they only want new members on their terms. This either means waiting an age before your view is sought or before you are allowed to do anything, or it means only wanting new people who will comfortably fit into the status quo.

New people inevitably mean new insights, new ideas, new experiences. The Church needs to be able to welcome this in the same way that the apostles welcomed Cleopas and his friend. The apostles are the ones marked out by Jesus for a special role of leadership in the Church, yet Jesus has appeared to these two renegades and entrusted them with the message of his resurrection and an explanation of the true meaning of Scripture.

A church community that wants to grow and wants to be welcoming is a church that wants to change and is prepared to share power, enabling the newest and the youngest and the least experienced to communicate the fresh word that God has for his Church in every age.

As Jesus arrives at Emmaus he makes as if to go on. But the two companions invite him to stay with them. At the heart of the story is this tentative invitation to spend more time with Jesus. And if the two companions had not implored Jesus to stay with them and share a meal, would he have given up on them? No, he would have walked the second and the third and the fourth mile at their side, still unrecognized but still faithfully accompanying them on the journey of their life, as Christians believe God accompanies every human person.

SPEAKING AND LISTENING

It is also worth reflecting on why they invited Jesus in. The reasons seem fairly obvious.

First, Jesus was a good listener. Although he had some tough things to say to them, he was happy to begin with their agenda and with their questions. He of all people knew what had been happening in Jerusalem these past few days, but he hears the story from their perspective, seeking to find out what is preventing them from really hearing what it is all about.

Being listened to is in itself a profound healing experience. The church that takes the Emmaus road story seriously will be a church wanting to listen well.

Secondly, when Jesus spoke he had something worth saying. These two people had heard everything that was necessary to understand the gospel – but at that moment it made no sense to them because they simply were not expecting a messiah who would suffer and die. Jesus does not offer them any new information, but by painstakingly going through the Scriptures offers them a radical new interpretation. Beginning with their questions he leads them to new understandings.

What a powerful combination: to listen well, and when you speak to have something worth saying. These are the qualities we need if we are to be effective in evangelism. When we speak it is not just to bombard people with information, but because we have listened well we are able to give new interpretations of their experience and lead them into fresh understandings of the Christian faith.

And we need to recognize that there is always more to know. Jesus makes as if to go on because Jesus is always leading us on. Love can always be deepened. The end of the journey is not commitment but discipleship. We need to grow in our relationship with God and with one another. The end of the journey is no earthly Jerusalem, not membership of the Church on earth, not even a heavenly Jerusalem, but God himself.

'I could see no temple in that city', writes St John, in his revelation of the heavenly Jerusalem, 'since the Lord God Almighty and the Lamb were themselves the temple.'

The road to Emmaus is the road to faith.

4

Starting-points – using *Emmaus* in your own church

Grand schemes are all very well but how (and where) do you actually begin? Every local church is different and there are many different ways of using *Emmaus* as a resource. This chapter gives you some ideas on getting started and Chapter 5 gives some examples of the different ways churches have used the material.

So how do you begin to build a way of initiating adults into the Christian faith which:

- is right for your situation

- is fully owned by the whole church

- integrates first contacts, nurture, ongoing discipleship and the worshipping life of the congregation?

Building this road to faith is not the work of a few weeks or months, but a commitment of several years (like the building of any major highway or bypass). Like road building, much of the real work is done at the stages of planning, preparation and laying the foundations. If the contractor comes along and puts down a neat layer of tarmac over a field it may look nice for a few weeks, but the lasting effects will be of no practical use. If planning permission is not obtained through the proper channels with due consultation with those affected, there will be little permanent progress. In some churches, you may find that many of the foundations and some of the building blocks for this high-way may already be in place. The *Emmaus* material will simply provide convenient tools for improving or widening or resurfacing what is already there. But in other churches there will be a feeling that you are starting very much from scratch and that the task is a large one. Several years of hard work may be needed before anything shows on the surface.

Beginning any new venture can be daunting. Help, advice and support are available. If you are in the United Kingdom, there are almost certainly churches in your area that are already using the material. The *Emmaus* authors and a group of trained consultants are available for training and help. Missioners in many denominations are familiar with the material and happy to help churches get started. Outside the United Kingdom there may still be someone locally who can help. Additional resources are available on the *Emmaus* website: www.natsoc.org.uk/emmaus.

If you believe it may be right to begin to use the *Emmaus* materials in a major way within your own church, as opposed to using a few of the materials here and there, then there are three separate stages you will need to move through. These are outlined below.

1	*Making the decision*
2	*Planning and preparation*
3	*Beginning the journey*

1 Making the decision

The decision to adopt *Emmaus* (or any other catechumenate model of initiation) needs to be made, as far as possible, by the whole church, because the whole life of the church will be affected. It is not a decision that any one individual can make by themselves.

Ideally as many people as possible need to read and digest this introductory book: at first in your main leadership and decision-making bodies, and then in the wider congregation. You may need to hold an introductory meeting open to everyone, spelling out this way of evangelism and initiation, possibly addressed by someone outside your own church. There will need to be an opportunity for prayer, reflection and discernment. Is this the right way forward for your own congregation at this particular time?

There are other good ways of going about evangelism and nurture. As a group we are not trying to say in any sense that *Emmaus* is the only way of engaging in this task. Often, *Emmaus* has been successfully combined with other material the church is already using.

You may want to consult with your denominational authority and seek its support. The final decision to go ahead needs to be made by the PCC or similar representative body in the church, after a considerable period of consultation, prayer and discussion.

St Mary's-by-the-Marsh is a traditional, middle-of-the-road Anglican church set in a residential suburb of a large town. The congregation numbers around 50 adults on a Sunday morning, mainly over 50 years of age, with a few more on the first Sunday of the month for the church parade service. The church has a number of traditional organizations, including a Mothers' Union, one housegroup run by the Reader (viewed with a little suspicion by some members of the church council) and a large number of social events. There is a part-time priest-in-charge, Mike Simpson, who is in his late 40s and has been in post for just over three years. He also has responsibility for a neighbouring parish, St John's-in-the-Wood. The church has been hesitant about evangelism for many years but thinks it 'ought to do something'. The vicar has traditionally run an adult confirmation class every two years or so as need arises. There is a tradition of ecumenical Lent groups.

Mike and one of the churchwardens first heard about Emmaus *at the Christian Resources Exhibition. They went to find out about a new sound system for the church but attended an introductory lecture while they were there. They both read the introductory book, were very excited by the possibilities and introduced the idea first to the standing committee and then to the PCC.*

The PCC agreed it was worth exploring and members agreed to buy for themselves a copy of the introductory book, which the secretary would order, to read it and pass it on to someone else. At the next meeting there was a longer discussion and again a green light was given. It was felt that more input was needed and the council agreed to invite the Diocesan Missioner, Father Tim Greenway, to come and speak to a meeting of the whole congregation.

The meeting, again, was well received. One or two members of the PCC had obtained other Emmaus *books and were keen to get going. Others were cautious and wanted to move more slowly. At Father Greenway's suggestion, the PCC met for a special hour of prayer before the next meeting, specifically to pray for discernment. There were no 'bolts from the blue' but people did find an emerging consensus and a growing sense of God's call to the parish to go down this road. Mike and the churchwardens had written to the bishop and the archdeacon about the initiative, and both had written very warm letters of encouragement, which were read out to the council. Meanwhile, a parallel process had been going on in St John's and the church councils were able to establish a joint planning group to take things forward.*

Five months after the initial contact at the Resources Exhibition the PCC voted unanimously to go ahead down the Emmaus *road and to move into the next period of planning and preparation.*

2   Planning and preparation

Once a decision has been made to go ahead, the temptation for many people is to leap into action and advertise the first course. In some cases this will be right, because much of the preparation has already happened. But in most, further planning and preparation will be required. This needs to happen over a number of months and should be in four different areas.

- *Teaching the whole congregation*
- *Creating space in the life of the church*
- *Prayer*
- *Practical planning*

TEACHING THE WHOLE CONGREGATION

As many of the congregation as possible need to become involved in learning that faith is a journey; in understanding the way adults come to faith today; in understanding the different elements in the *Emmaus* process; and in thinking through the ministry of sponsors, the place of special services and so on.

This learning can happen in a number of different ways: over a series of different evening meetings; over a special weekend's introduction to *Emmaus*; through articles in a parish magazine; through sessions in existing groups and organizations. If the whole congregation is to be involved in the work of mission and welcome, then this preparation and teaching must not be skipped over.

As part of this teaching and preparation some churches may want to run an *Emmaus* nurture course especially for existing church members and potential sponsors. This can be useful in many ways. It enables a significant group of people within the congregation to look at the foundations of their faith again. It gives the leaders of the course a 'dry run' with Christians rather than enquirers. It enables the church leaders to work through the material in some detail; to change or adapt different sessions – to get a feel for the course.

Providing the first pilot course goes well, if this is fed back to the wider congregation, there may then be an enthusiasm for drawing others in the first time round. At least one church, which already had several home groups, used the nurture material as a basis for a series of sermons for the whole congregation to work through.

CREATING SPACE IN THE LIFE OF THE CHURCH

Many churches are very busy places. Even small congregations can draw in and use up all the available energy of clergy and lay people in just keeping things going.

But effective, ongoing mission and outreach can only happen where there is space, time and energy in the life of the clergy and the people. If the *Emmaus* materials are simply bolted on to the life of a church that is already over-busy maintaining itself, then there will be very little fruit, just frustration and tiredness. There needs to be a conscious, deliberate attempt in the period of preparation to simplify the life of the congregation and to do less. The whole basis of *Emmaus* is taking time to be with people. Clergy and lay people alike may need to thin out their busy lives so that there is time and space again to walk alongside those who are going in the wrong direction, as Jesus did.

Thinning out and simplifying the life of the church is not easy. Many of us justify our whole lives by how busy we are and how much we have to do. A busy church, we think, must be a fruitful church – just look at how much is going on! Jesus' picture of the vine reminds us that a key part of bearing fruit is being willing to be pruned. No one can prescribe for anyone else how that pruning is to happen – but it is a very necessary part of any person or congregation becoming effective in mission.

PRAYER

1 Corinthians 3 is a wonderful chapter of the Bible on evangelism, nurture and growth. In it Paul writes: 'I planted, Apollos watered, but God gave the growth.' Making contact, forming relationships, sharing faith, nurture, enabling people to grow are all, at one level, human activities. But they are also, and more importantly, God's activity and work in human lives. And that means that we ourselves need to develop a sense of working in partnership with the Holy Spirit (and one in which we

are the very junior partners). The only way in which that can happen is through prayer.

The ways in which each church begins to pray for its ongoing life of mission and initiation will vary enormously. In some there will be special services and intercessions; in others meetings for open prayer; in others again special prayer cards; opportunities to fast; half-nights or days of prayer. The form does not matter. The prayer itself is essential.

PRACTICAL PLANNING

This is perhaps the easiest area. It is best done by a small group appointed for the task, which should almost certainly include the priest or minister responsible for the church, and senior lay leaders. The kinds of questions the planning group will need to answer in the early stages of involvement with *Emmaus* are these:

How will we handle the 'contact' material?

- Will there be a study course or day?

- How can it be introduced to different groups?

- Should there be a PCC sub-committee?

- Who will be responsible for this area?

What about the nurture group?

- When will the first group meet?

  Arranging evangelism nurture groups is always a venture of faith. Don't wait until you have twelve enquirers — otherwise you will wait forever. Plan the group well in advance, in faith that God will provide at least some people to be part of it.

- Who will the leaders be?

45

- Where will it meet?

  Comfortable, accessible surroundings, please!

- Will the leaders need training and preparation and if so, where will that come from?

  Can the denomination or diocese help?

- Will you involve sponsors?

  If so, who will they be and what will they do? How will you communicate their role?

- How will you advertise the group?

  Where do you think the people will come from?

- Will you use the special services?

  What forms of the services will you use? How many will you include and at what points in the journey? Will these be in the main Sunday services?

- How will confirmation and receiving communion fit in?

Help in thinking through these questions can be found in the *Emmaus* books and *Leading an Emmaus Groups*, the nurture course Leaders' Guide.

What about the growth material?

- Will you go for ongoing groups or occasional courses?

- In either case, who will be the leaders?

- How will the leaders themselves be supported?

It sounds a lot to think about. But the answers to most of the questions should not be too difficult to work out for your own situation.

When you have hammered out a practical plan together, take it to the PCC and discuss it some more. Show it to someone outside your own congregation and ask them to comment. Build in any suggestions or improvements. And be prepared to change and adapt as you go along.

St Mary's and St John's congregations got on well with the teaching and learning side of the preparation. There had not been much systematic teaching in the church for years. Father Greenway came back to lead around 25 people through an introductory weekend. On the Friday evening people looked together at contact; on Saturday morning at nurture; and on Saturday afternoon at growth. Father Greenway preached at a combined Sunday morning Eucharist which was a significant milestone in the life of the parishes.

Following the special weekend, the existing housegroup began straight away to engage with the Emmaus growth material, beginning with 'Living the Gospel', followed by the 'Personal Identity' module from the growth section. The life of the group almost immediately took on a new purpose and direction and one or two new members joined. The Reader began to liaise much more closely with Mike about what was happening.

The PCC decided to call their nurture course 'Christians for Life' and opted to run a pilot course for the two congregations which Mike led with one co-leader from each church. Ten people came, two of whom were on the fringe of St Mary's, and one member, brought by his wife, was not a regular attender. The group took a few weeks to get going, but it went really well. Everyone, including the leaders, took new steps into the Christian faith and life. The person who rarely came to church began attending regularly and asked to be confirmed. Others too began attending more regularly. At the end of the course the group wanted to stay together and look at some of the growth materials. The lay leaders took them on. They began with 'God the Father'.

So far, so good. Thinning out the life of the church proved more difficult. After a great deal of debate and some controversy, the St John's PCC agreed to cancel their summer fair and winter bazaar. This had financial implications as well as social ones. The social secretary resigned from the PCC in protest. The PCC of St Mary's voted to meet six times a year instead of eleven. Again the decision was not unanimous and was to be reviewed after a year. St Mary's choir and the Mothers' Union were both in favour of Emmaus, but became concerned when Mike stopped popping in to choir practice altogether and only came to the Mothers' Union once every two months – and then not for the whole meeting. One or two forward-thinking people actually suggested that the parishes employ a part-time secretary so that Mike would not have to spend three mornings a week on administration and correspondence. This idea was defeated but someone volunteered to give a morning a week on a voluntary basis.

Neither church had any tradition of meeting together for prayer outside Sunday services. Cautiously the planning group suggested a weekly hour of prayer on Saturday mornings in Lent. Only two or three people came – but it was a beginning and the practice continued after Easter. Two-hour prayer vigils were held on the evening before major festivals. These were very simple services with opportunity for silent and extemporary prayer to be offered. A spirituality was beginning to grow up around the church's vision for mission.

The planning group concluded that the churches should not use the contact material as a separate stage, but should instead gradually develop different methods of making contact appropriate to each parish. This ongoing question was referred back to the PCCs.

Mike himself did most of the planning for 'Christians for Life' and opted to lead the groups himself, with different co-leaders each time. He rang colleagues in neighbouring parishes who were taking part in the Emmaus course on a number of occasions. The parish decided to use 'informal' sponsors who would support in prayer but would not have to come to the meetings. People were nervous about the special services but agreed to give them a try, providing they were optional to all the participants. Material from the growth section of the course was to be used in ongoing groups with perhaps some occasional courses. Some longer standing members of the PCC were sceptical about this.

Altogether the period of planning and preparation took just over a year from the PCC's decision to go ahead with Emmaus. *The first full nurture group was planned to start in three months' time.*

3 Beginning the journey

Providing the preparation and planning have gone well, making a formal beginning should be fairly straightforward (in so far as anything ever is). Most churches will be best following St Mary's route: not running a separate group for contact, but beginning to offer a regular group for evangelism and nurture.

The pattern with nurture groups is normally one of small beginnings: a trickle rather than a flood of enquirers. It is important to be faithful and work with whoever comes, even if they do not appear to be the most promising bunch of new converts you have ever seen. Normally you will find that the next group is slightly larger and more promising, and, providing the church is continuing to work on contact, the trickle becomes a steady stream over a number of years. A common mistake churches have made with the *Emmaus* material is to plan, expect or take on too much too soon, which is not then sustained.

Whenever something is done for the first time, whether it is a coffee morning, a nurture group or a service of welcome, it will be important to stop and reflect on what has happened and to learn lessons from it, both positive and negative.

As you move along the road with the *Emmaus* material and the congregation begins to grow, you will need to give particular thought to how to cope with and care for larger numbers of people. If this is to happen through a network of small groups, then think through how the leaders are to be identified, cared for and supported. If the caring is to be through pastoral visiting, begin to prepare and plan for who the visitors might be and how the work is to be divided.

St Mary's and St John's first full 'Christians for Life' group attracted six people, who, with the leaders, made a group of nine. Three of the group had come into contact with the churches through baptisms, weddings or funerals; one person had moved into the area and been brought by a neighbour, and two existing members of St John's joined in. The group enjoyed being together and the four new members took part, very nervously, in the first service of welcome at the end of Part One of the course. The other special services all went well. Three of the group were confirmed by the bishop in a neighbouring parish and the other three renewed their baptismal vows at the same service. The group stayed together, with the co-leaders, and began the growth material with the course on prayer.

Meanwhile at St Mary's the PCC contact group and the Mothers' Union had joined forces to begin a parent and toddler group for the area, together with a crèche on Sundays and a lay-led baptism preparation team. St Mary's was suddenly in touch with young families again. St John's began a simple door-to-door visiting scheme, making real contact with its parish again for the first time in years. Mike and the new pastoral team spent some of his freed-up evenings visiting the new contacts, and several of them were thinking hard about coming to the next 'Christians for Life' course. The existing homegroup, after working through 'Living the Gospel', was beginning to see family, friends and colleagues becoming interested in the faith. A single man began coming to church after the group organized a bowling evening and supper. He too was keen to come to 'Christians for Life'.

By the time the second full nurture group began, three groups were meeting and working their way through growth courses. Mike met the group leaders once a month and was in touch with them more often on the telephone. Members of the PCC had already been asked by Father Greenway to share their experiences of Emmaus *with other churches in the diocese. The local Methodists were beginning a similar scheme — so was the Roman Catholic parish across the town — and they were using* Emmaus *as well.*

50

Now that growth really was beginning, most of the old difficulties and grumbles in the churches had subsided — but new ones took their place. Noisy babies disturbed the peace of the Eucharist at St John's. There were real elections for the PCC in St Mary's. Some of the more traditional people felt left out in both places. But they were, at least, problems of growth not stagnation. The majority of the congregation was on board and the church sensed God's guiding hand on its life. Most of all, it was possible to say, year by year, that the Lord was adding to their number those who were being saved.

Many adults in today's generation have a belief in God and a desire to know him. The risen Lord Jesus himself seeks to draw near to them, to walk with them, to teach them, to reveal himself to them and to commission them to go.

We invite you to join with us in the wonderful work of making disciples.

5

How is *Emmaus* being used?[1]

Since its launch in autumn 1996 over 50,000 books have been sold in the *Emmaus* series, including 8,000 copies of the nurture course, and it has had a positive impact on thousands of churches throughout Britain and in other parts of the world: to our knowledge courses have been run in South Carolina, Philadelphia, Dublin  and South Africa. This, along with the fact that *Emmaus* is starting to be translated into other languages (Welsh, German and several African languages), demonstrates the wide scope of the course. It has been tailored for use, by lay and ordained, in a variety of contexts – church-based and non-church-based – in ways that demonstrate the flexibility of *Emmaus* and the creativity of those implementing the material. Many people have commented on the nature of the teaching style underpinning the series: the group discussions, the potential for openness and informality, and the accessibility and versatility of the material. The nature of the programme has resulted in nurture groups developing into housegroups, and often providing leaders and sponsors for new nurture courses. It has been used to help people explore faith from a variety of different stages on the journey of faith, older Christians learning alongside those who are beginning to explore issues of Christian belief, spirituality and lifestyle. Personal accounts from some of those who have participated in *Emmaus* courses demonstrate the substantive impact it is having on people's lives.

1 A variety of contexts

Emmaus has been adopted by a wide range of Anglican churches, and a number of other denominations. A Baptist minister writes:

> *Emmaus* has proved an invaluable resource for deepening faith and the challenge to active discipleship. Its open approach has proved accessible for both old and young, for new as well as mature Christians. It has fostered committed but inquiring discipleship, both personal and corporate.

Reports from groups using the course show it is implemented across a range of churchmanship, located in both rural and urban contexts. A deanery in St Albans Diocese reports that

> churches in the deanery, ranging from charismatic evangelical to Anglo-Catholic, are using, or are about to use, one or more stages of the *Emmaus* material.[2]

Another indication of the broad scope of *Emmaus* is the way it has been used with young and old, committed Christians and enquirers. A youth group in the Wakefield Diocese took up the suggestion in the course that sponsors should directly participate. The result was a wide range of people, bringing a variety of life experiences to the course, enabling everyone to go over the basics and learn together.

Emmaus has been used in some churches to inject new life into housegroups, as well as form nurture groups. Between autumn 1996 and autumn 1998, one parish successfully introduced a nurture group aimed at people on the fringes, which also attracted some long-standing members of the church who wanted a confirmation refresher course. This group developed into a housegroup in its own right. Members of the group were encouraged to help in welcome evenings and to contact people they thought might be interested in *Emmaus*. This church now has a young people's group, a morning group and a new evening group about to start. Having completed the nurture course, the youth group chose to continue as a group using one of the growth courses, 'Growing in the Scriptures'. Established housegroups, numbering over 70 people, were encouraged to trial *Emmaus* material and then decide as individual groups if they wished to continue using it. All the housegroups felt that going with *Emmaus* was the right option for the church. This example highlights the different applications of the course within one parish.

Another parish reports that they used *Emmaus* to re-launch a small housegroup that was struggling to find its focus. The group became a welcoming group of sponsors for a number of enquirers. The result was a hospitable and open nurture group that is reported to have benefited newcomers and the original members of the group.

Emmaus is also proving a useful resource in non-church-based contexts. In an outer-city council estate in Hull, the Longhill Link-up Trust (a Church of England sponsored project) provides a drop-in centre for a chat over a cup of coffee, or to buy second-hand clothes. The minister in charge of the project introduced a lunchtime evangelistic *Emmaus* course over ten sessions for twelve project volunteers, of whom three could not read or write. However, the material proved to be adaptable. He writes:

> *Emmaus* is completely and utterly participatory. There are very good questions and a lot of evangelism was done in the groups, through talking. *Emmaus* works well with people because it assumes nothing, you don't need to know anything, it's like starting with a blank piece of paper. *Emmaus* has absolutely fantastic logic – the sessions are linked and can be summarized, and all the sessions work together.[3]

Autumn 2000 saw the piloting of an online *Emmaus* course at www.allbelievers.org. Participation in the *Emmaus* Internet trial offered access to a special web site where learning material will be posted regularly. With this came the opportunity to reflect on a variety of texts and issues and participate in online discussion.

Emmaus has proved a useful resource in schools. An example from Dublin demonstrates how the material can be adapted for use in religious education lessons where it has provided a 'good entry level for work with children from varying backgrounds'[4].

2   The flexibility of *Emmaus*

A report from Nottinghamshire demonstrates the flexibility of the course in that two different parishes, one a middle-class suburban area and another a working-class UPA parish, were able to access *Emmaus* 'according to our individual situation, and the material seemed well suited to this. It led very gently from the personal to the spiritual, encouraging deeper and deeper insights.'[5] This resulted in ten adults being confirmed and another twenty people preparing to start the journey. *Emmaus* is also being used in housegroups within these parishes.

A youth group leader using *Emmaus* comments:

> Though the course appears very simple and straightforward, its flexibility and the spaces that it leaves for development and insight mean that you can go as far as is appropriate for the group.[6]

A leader, having completed 'Growing in the Scriptures' with a cell group of eight to twelve people, comments that the format of the *Emmaus* notes is 'sufficient to give the confidence to guide and direct the group but not so comprehensive that no-one would have enough time for preparation'. This person also comments on how the structure of the notes allows for flexibility according to the needs of a particular group. She continues:

> In a group with an immense range of ability and experience everybody has found something of value and interest. It has certainly helped to bind the group members together as we feel we have a common purpose in exploring the faith. It has

> allowed people to proceed at their own pace and
> not made differences in understanding or back-
> ground a difficulty.[7]

This view finds support in the following comment from an Anglican
priest in County Durham: 'the questions are designed so they can be
answered at very different levels, from a simple and straightforward
level to a difficult and complex level. They are clear without being
patronising.'[8]

3 The creativity of those implementing the material

Some churches have chosen to build the group meetings around a
shared meal. In at least one instance this led to the production of a book
of recipes, interspersed with comments from participants about their
view of the course. One such comment from a member of Table Talk
(the name of this *Emmaus* group) reads:

> Table Talk provided an opportunity for two-way
> dialogue that the traditional Sunday service is
> unable to deliver. Much of the time was spent
> discussing everyday life and experiences with
> familiar faces, over sumptuous food and wine.[9]

This group reports that a key benefit of including a meal in the meeting is that it creates a more informal atmosphere: 'People chatted and
got to know each other and so the course wasn't so intimidating.'[10]

Another parish choosing to include a meal commented that 'eating
together was a great way to unwind and get to know each other properly. This meant that it then felt quite natural to discuss our lives and
the Christian faith with each other.'[11]

4 The nature of the teaching style underpinning the series

Almost all groups feeding back about their experiences of *Emmaus* have commented on the effectiveness of the teaching style underpinning the series. The collaborative model, focused on people working together, sharing, discussing, posing questions, is proving effective. A youth leader writes:

> It enabled people, through buzz groups, to find out for themselves and then to have what they had discovered confirmed. I believe this is a far more effective way to teach than simply 'telling'.[12]

This point is borne out in the following observation from a young person:

> I had been a Christian for nine months when our youth group started the *Emmaus* course, but I'd never experienced anything like this before. Because most of us were new to this idea, and to each other, the way the course works – with small group discussions mixed in with teaching – was ideal as we were able to talk through our opinions and not just be 'preached' at.[13]

The benefit of such a collaborative approach is highlighted in the following statement from a member of an *Emmaus* course:

> The people I started on the *Emmaus* course with are all at different stages of their belief but are still able to learn from each other . . .[14]

John Morison, while Diocesan Missioner in Derby, commented on how *Emmaus* allows people to work in a relaxed and unpressured way, which acknowledges people's experiences and 'enables participants to follow at their own pace'. He continues:

> Ordinary church members often express the desire
> to learn more about the Faith, but are not sure
> exactly how to go about it. Most find that it's more
> fun learning together . . . I have found that it is
> theologically and educationally sound, attractively
> presented and easy to adapt to your precise
> situation.[15]

Jerry Lepine, Southwark Diocesan Missioner, summing up reports he
has received concerning *Emmaus*, states that he found that '*Emmaus*
affirmed and built on what was already going on in parishes as well as
offering a way into evangelism and nurture which was non-threatening.
The strategy made sense because it connected with the way Christians
experienced their faith.'[16] Contributors to *Table Talk*,[17] the recipe book
referred to above, comment in ways that bear out Lepine's view:

> . . . openness, warm welcome, acceptance, patience.

> Everybody's view is important, even if it isn't the
> same as the 'established view'.

> Learning with others keeps the content in language
> that I understand and relate to.

5   Personal accounts

The following quotations are from people who have experienced
Emmaus:

> The wonderful teaching of *Emmaus* is that 'God
> meets you where you are'. This has been proved to
> me in that we, the group members at different
> stages in our faith, have come together and been
> able to grow alongside each other. We have shared
> the best we can and I feel very privileged to be a
> part of that. I have come to believe and accept that
> my best is good enough, for now . . . *Emmaus* has

helped me to see what I needed to see. God has been with me many times in the past . . . *Emmaus* has been very important in my journey to know God and to help me form a stronger, closer relationship with him.[18]

As a relatively new Christian, I thought the course would be full of things I already knew – but I learnt so much from it . . . The simple way *Emmaus* teaches Christianity reached me and made me reconsider everything I had sunk into accepting. Because of this, by the end of the six weeks I was ready to recommit my life and receive the Holy Spirit. I thought this wouldn't affect me much, but I really felt God's presence and since then have heard him a great deal more. *Emmaus* also encouraged me to read the Bible and pray, things which I was rapidly leaving behind in my life.[19]

When you start coming to church it's easy to be fooled into believing that everyone else sitting in their pews on a Sunday has got all this faith stuff sorted out. Very few people have the courage to question or express doubts in case they look foolish. It's only when you make time to question and face up to the doubts that you can really start to make sense of this elusive thing called faith, and the *Emmaus* course provides a secure place for everybody to do this.[20]

My study with the *Emmaus* Group led me to explore my inner self, to find my place in the world alongside other people. I came to realize that I wasn't the only person thinking and worrying about religion and belief. Together we helped each other to take a few steps forward along the journey of faith. Without the opportunity to study together I would not have been able to listen to sermons in this new way, nor would I have grown spiritually or had the courage to go to a prayer conference or even read the Bible . . . The *Emmaus* Group was the turning point, a stepping stone which has helped me to accept God into my life and shown me how to grow both spiritually and physically into a better person.[21]

A versatile resource, *Emmaus* has helped churches to contact new people, run nurture courses, rejuvenate housegroups, explore issues of Christian belief, spirituality and lifestyle, and develop more open relationships between people. It has been and continues to be used practically and flexibly in a variety of contexts in ways that are positively affecting the lives of individuals and communities.

No matter how long you have been a Christian you are never too young or too old to learn about Jesus, if you are willing to listen. Why don't you give it a try?[22]

Notes

1   Chapter 5 has been largely compiled by Kate Bruce from a range of material gathered by the authors and publishers.

2   *Using Emmaus: Our Story So Far*, pamphlet from St Mary, Marshalwick, St Albans, 1998, p. 1.

3   *Emmaus Newsletter*, Issue No. 3.

4   http://www.natsoc.org.uk/emmaus/tips.htm 01/08/00

5   *Emmaus Newsletter*, Issue No. 2.

6   Cathy Preston, *Emmaus Report from Slaithwaite Youth Group*, 1997.

7   Jenny Cheesbrough, *Using the Emmaus Growth Modules in Cell Groups*, published by St Thomas, Huddersfield, 1998.

8   *Emmaus Newsletter*, Issue No. 3.

9   *Table Talk*, published by Holy Trinity Church, Clapham, 1997.

10   *Emmaus Newsletter*, Issue No. 3.

11   http://www.natsoc.org.uk/emmaus/church_stories.htm 01/08/00

12   Cathy Preston, *Emmaus Report from Slaithwaite Youth Group*.

13   Rachel Bagshaw, *Emmaus Newsletter,* Issue No. 1.

14   Jillian Baldam.

15   Derby Diocesan Paper, January 1997.

16   Paper from Southwark Diocese, 1997.

17   *Table Talk*, published by Holy Trinity Church, Clapham, 1997.

18   Anonymous Christian from Wakefield, *Emmaus Newsletter*, Issue No. 2.

19   Rachel Bagshaw, *Emmaus Newsletter*, Issue No. 1.

20   Jackie Dawn, in *The Way of Renewal*, A Report by the Board of Mission of the General Synod of the Church of England, Church House Publishing, 1998, p.101.

21   Eleanor Crossley, in *The Way of Renewal*, A Report by the Board of Mission of the General Synod of the Church of England, Church House Publishing, 1998, p.101.

22   Jillian Baldam.

Further reading

William Abraham, *The Logic of Evangelism*, Hodder & Stoughton, 1989

Peter Ball and Malcolm Grundy, *Faith on the Way: A Practical Parish Guide to the Adult Catechumenate*, Mowbray, 2000

Called to New Life: The World of Lay Discipleship, Church House Publishing, 1999

Stephen Cottrell, *Sacrament, Wholeness and Evangelism*, Grove Booklets, 1996

Stephen Cottrell and Steven Croft, *Travelling Well: a companion guide to the Christian faith*, Church House Publishing, 2000

Yvonne Craig, *Learning for Life: A handbook of Adult Religious Education*, Mowbray, 1994

Christine Dodd, *Making RCIA work*, Geoffrey Chapman, 1993

John Finney, *Finding Faith Today*, Bible Society, 1992

Nicky Gumbel, *Telling Others: The Alpha Initiative*, Kingsway, 1994

On the Way: Towards an Integrated Approach to Christian Initiation, Church House Publishing, 1995

Robert Warren, *Being Human, Being Church*, Marshall Pickering, 1995

Robert Warren, *Building Missionary Congregations*, Church House Publishing, 1995

The Emmaus web site: www.natsoc.org.uk/emmaus

The authors

STEPHEN COTTRELL is a member of the Springboard Team, the initiative in evangelism of the Archbishops of Canterbury and York, and was, until recently, the Wakefield Diocesan Missioner. He is editor and co-author of *Follow Me*, a programme of Christian nurture based on the catechumenate that is widely used by Anglo-Catholic churches. He has also written *Praying Through Life* and, with Steven Croft, the handbook *Travelling Well*.

STEVEN CROFT is Warden of Cranmer Hall within St John's College, Durham. He was previously Vicar of Ovenden in Halifax for nine years and Mission Consultant in the Diocese of Wakefield. He is the author of the handbooks *Growing New Christians* and *Making New Disciples*, and his work has pioneered understanding of the relationship between evangelism and nurture. His recent work includes *Ministry in Three Dimensions: Ordination and Leadership in the Local Church*.

JOHN FINNEY was, until recently, Bishop of Pontefract and was also Decade for Evangelism Officer for the Church of England. His report *Finding Faith Today* has been instrumental in helping the Church understand how people become Christians. He was also involved in the writing of *On the Way – Towards an Integrated Approach to Christian Initiation* for General Synod.

FELICITY LAWSON has been Dean of Ministry and Director of Ordinands in the Diocese of Wakefield. Together with John Finney she wrote *Saints Alive*, a nurture course helping Christians towards a deeper understanding of life in the Spirit. She has recently returned to parochial ministry.

ROBERT WARREN was Team Rector of one of the largest and fastest growing churches in England, St Thomas, Crookes. He succeeded John Finney as the Church of England's National Officer for Evangelism. His book *Building Missionary Congregations* sees the catechumenate as one of the potential ways for facilitating the change required as we move from inherited patterns of church life towards the emerging models that will shape the Church in the new millennium. He is now working full time as a member of the Springboard Team.

Although all five authors are Anglicans, the *Emmaus* material can be used by any denomination and has been produced with this in mind.

Travelling Well

A companion guide to the Christian Faith

Stephen Cottrell and Steven Croft
£6.95   0 7151 4935 0

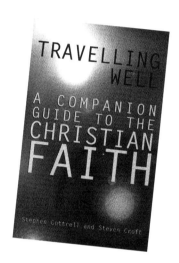

A guide for Christians who
are setting out on their journey
of faith as well as for more
experienced travellers.
Travelling Well provides help
and instruction in important
areas of the Christian life such as
prayer, reading the Bible, relating
faith to daily life and sharing our
faith. Each chapter explores a
theme and has a selection of
readings and prayers.

Stephen Cottrell and Steven Croft are two of the authors of *Emmaus:
The Way of Faith* and are both well known in the field of adult initiation
and discipleship.

> 'This is a book full of bite-size
> chunks of practical Christian
> counsel – yet it is never lightweight.'
>
> **Revd Stephen Lynas, MBE**

Praying Through Life

Stephen Cottrell
£7.95   0 7151 4902 4

Aimed at those starting out
in the Christian faith and at
all who find prayer difficult,
or want to journey deeper in
their faith. The book begins
with an introduction on
'What is prayer?' and has
sections on how to pray in
different situations. It ends
with ten golden rules for
prayer and a section on
prayer and evangelism.

'*Praying through* Life
stands out for its practical,
honest and accessible
content.'

ACT